A NOTE TO PARENTS

Reading is often considered the most important skill children learn in the primary grades. Much can be done at home to lay the foundation for early reading success.

When they read, children use the following to figure out words: story and picture clues, how a word is used in a sentence, and sound/spelling relationships. The **Hello Reader!** *Phonics Fun* series focuses on sound/spelling relationships through phonics activities. Phonics instruction unlocks the door to understanding sounds and the letters or spelling patterns that represent them.

The **Hello Reader!** *Phonics Fun* series is divided into the following three sets of books, based on important phonic elements:
- **Sci-Fi Phonics**: word families
- **Monster Phonics**: consonants, blends, and digraphs
- **Funny Tale Phonics**: short and long vowels

Learn About Vowels

The Funny Tale Phonics stories, including *The Red Hen*, feature words that have the same vowel sound. These books help children become aware of and use these sounds when decoding, or sounding out, new words. After reading the book, you might wish to begin lists of words that contain each vowel sound. For example, one list could contain all the short *e* words, another list all the short *o* words, and so on.

Enjoy the Activities
- Challenge your child to build words using the letters and word parts provided. Help your child by demonstrating how to sound out new words.
- Match words with pictures to help your child attach meaning to text.
- Become word detectives by identifying story words with the same vowel sound.
- Keep the activities game-like and praise your child's efforts.

Develop Fluency

Encourage your child to read these books again and again and again. Each time, set a different purpose for reading.
- Point to a word in the story. Say it aloud. Ask your child what sound he or she hears in the middle of the word. Then look at the letter or letters that stand for that sound.
- Suggest to your child that he or she read the book to a friend, family member, or even a pet.

Whatever you do, have fun with the books and instill the joy of reading in your child. It is one of the most important things you can do!

—Wiley Blevins, Reading Specialist
Ed.M., Harvard University

W9-ARL-742

To my most lovely Genevieve
— J.B.S.

To my wife, Martha
— R.F.

No part of this publication may be reproduced, or stored in a retrieval system, or trans-mitted in any form or by any means, electronic, mechanical, photocopying, recording, or otherwise, without written permission of the publisher. For information regarding per-missions, write to Scholastic Inc., Attention: Permissions Department, 555 Broadway, New York, NY 10012.

Text copyright © 1998 by Judith Bauer Stamper.
Illustrations copyright © 1998 by Ron Fritz.
All rights reserved. Published by Scholastic Inc.
HELLO READER!, CARTWHEEL BOOKS and associated logos
are trademarks and/or registered trademarks of Scholastic Inc.

Library of Congress Cataloging-in-Publication Data
Stamper, Judith Bauer.
    The red hen / by Judith Bauer Stamper; illustrated by Ron Fritz;
phonics activities by Wiley Blevins.
        p.   cm.—(Hello reader! Phonics fun. Funny tale phonics)
    "Vowels: short e, short o, and short u."
    "Cartwheel books."
    Summary: Lazy Fox and Duck are in for a big surprise after they refuse to
help the hardworking Little Red Hen prepare lunch.
    Includes related phonics activities.
    ISBN 0-590-76269-9
    [1. Folklore.]   I. Fritz, Ronald, ill.   II. Blevins, Wiley.   III. Little Red Hen.
IV. Title.   V. Series.
PZ8.1.S786Li   1998
398.24'528625
[E] — dc21
                                                                        97-23398
                                                                            CIP
                                                                             AC

10 9 8 7 6 5 4 3   8 9/9 0/0 01 02

Printed in the U.S.A. 24
First printing, May 1998

The Red Hen

by Judith Bauer Stamper
Illustrated by Ron Fritz
Phonics Activities by Wiley Blevins

Hello Reader! Phonics Fun

Funny Tale Phonics • Vowels: short *e*, short *o*, and short *u*

SCHOLASTIC INC. Cartwheel BOOKS®

New York Toronto London Auckland Sydney

Once there was a peppy red hen.
She cleaned her house again
and again.

"Peck, Peck, Peck!
This house is a wreck!"

One day the hen walked two blocks
to see the duck and the fox.

"Cluck, Cluck, Cluck!
What a lazy fox and duck!"

"Hi, Red Hen.
Welcome to our pen."

"I came to ask you over for lunch.
Can you help me make some food
to munch?"

"Not I," said the fox.
"I'm sorting my socks."

"Not I," said the duck.
"I'm fixing my truck."

The peppy red hen went back home.
She made some dough all alone.

"Sob, Sob, Sob!
I always do the job!

"I still need help making lunch.
Can you pick some tomatoes
for us to munch?"

"Not I," said the fox.
"I'm building my blocks."

"Not I," said the duck.
"My foot is stuck."

The peppy red hen went back home.
She picked the tomatoes all alone.

"Sob, Sob, Sob!
I always do the job!

"I still need help making lunch.
Can you chop some cheese
for us to munch?"

"Not I," said the fox.
"I'm filling this box."

"Not I," said the duck.
"You're out of luck."

The peppy red hen went back home.
She chopped the cheese all alone.

"Sob, Sob, Sob!
I always do the job!"

"Hi! We're here for lunch.
What do you have for us to munch?"

"Cluck, Cluck, Cluck!
Fox and Duck,
   you are both out of luck!

"I worked hard to make this yummy.
And now it's going in MY tummy!"

• PHONICS ACTIVITIES •
Sound Sort

Find the items in each animal's home.
What has the same sound as the *e* in *hen*?

What has the same sound as the *o* in *fox*?
What has the same sound as the *u* in *duck*?

Picture Match

Use one of the letters below to finish each name. Then match the picture with its name. Find the picture's name in the story.

o   **e**   **u**

h _ n

s _ c k

t r _ c k

b l _ c k

b _ x

Word Search

Find each picture's name in the word search.

h	e	n	d	k
f	i	d	u	s
i	x	h	c	o
c	b	f	k	c
b	l	o	c	k
b	o	x	s	o

Word Ladders

Use one of the words in the box to finish each word ladder. Each word on the ladder changes by only one letter.

luck   hot

not   hen

mop

hop

net

nut

duck

lock

ten

pen

Build a Word

Use the letters in the blocks to make new words. Add each letter to the incomplete word. If it makes a word, say it aloud.

b_g   p_p   c_p

l_ck   h_t   b_d

n_t   d_ck   l_g

Answers

Sound Sort

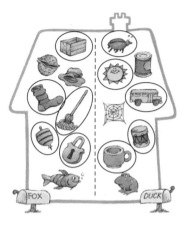

Picture Match

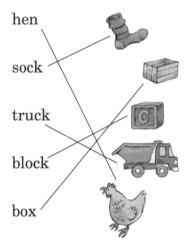

hen

sock

truck

block

box

Word Ladders

mop
hop
hot

net
not
nut

duck
luck
lock

hen
ten
pen

Word Search

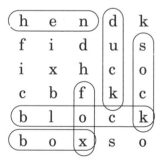

h	e	n	d	k
f	i	d	u	s
i	x	h	c	o
c	b	f	k	c
b	l	o	c	k
b	o	x	s	o

Build a Word

beg bog bug; pep pop pup; cop cup;
lock luck; hot hut; bed bud;
net not nut; deck dock duck; leg log lug